HEATHCLIFF DINES OUT

The funniest feline in America delights millions of fans every day as he appears in over 1000 newspapers. You'll have a laugh a minute as Heathcliff tangles with the milkman, the fish store owner, the tuna fisherman and just about everyone else he runs into. If you're looking for some fun, look no farther. Heathcliff is here.

Heathcliff Books

HEATHCLIFF®
DINES OUT

by

CHARTER BOOKS, NEW YORK

Cartoons previously published in
Wicked Loving Heathcliff

HEATHCLIFF DINES OUT

A Charter Book / published by arrangement with
McNaught Syndicate, Inc., and DIC Audiovisuel, Inc.

PRINTING HISTORY
Charter Original / February 1985
Special Book Club edition / October 1987

Charter Books are published by The Berkley Publishing Group,
200 Madison Avenue, New York, New York 10016.
The name "CHARTER" and the "C" logo
are trademarks belonging to Charter Communications, Inc.

PRINTED IN THE UNITED STATES OF AMERICA

"HOOD ORNAMENT?!...I DON'T HAVE A HOOD ORNAMENT!!"

"SONJA'S NOT MUCH OF A MOUSER!"

"IT'S PUBLIC ENEMY NO. 1!... 'BABYFACE NUTMEG'!"

"SINCE WHEN DID WE BECOME A BOOK CRITIC?!"

"...AND GUESS WHO'S ON THE ORGAN?"

"LOOKS LIKE I'M NOT GOING ANYWHERE!"

"HE WON'T DO 'BRAND X'... ONLY THE STARRING ROLE!"

" VALENTINES FROM CRAZY SHIRLEY. "

"HE'S CONDUCTING FIELD TRIPS FOR THE YOUNGSTERS!"

"TONIGHT, I'M AFRAID HE'S DOING 'OKLAHOMA'!"

"CRAZY SHIRLEY SWIPED MY NET!"

"IN THE FOURTEENTH CENTURY, IT SEEMS THERE WAS ONE 'HEATHCLIFF, THE ROYAL MOUSER'!"

"I THOUGHT YOU'D LIKE A NEW BONNET!"

"WELL, IF IT ISN'T CAPTAIN AHAB
IN SEARCH OF MOBY DICK!"

"FASTEST TONGUE IN THE WEST!"

"YES, HEATHCLIFF.....I'VE SEEN YOUR X-RAYS MANY, MANY TIMES!"

"I THINK YOU'VE HAD ENOUGH!"

"DON'T WORRY ABOUT
CRAZY SHIRLEY..."

"...SHE JUMPS OFF
HERE ALL THE TIME."

"THERE'S A CAT BACK THERE
WITH A DRILL AND A STRAW!"

"OH, LOOK!...HE ENJOYED HIS SARDINES!"

"HMMM ?...THEY'RE TEN MINUTES OVERDUE!"

"COME BACK WITH THAT FLOUNDER!"

" CASANOVA....

....IS HERE."

"THE CHAMP IS COMING IN FOR A WORKOUT!"

"YOUR FATHER ISN'T ALLOWED VISITORS....
HE'S IN SOLITARY."

"YOU SHOULDN'T MESS WITH A JUNKYARD DOG!"

"PUT BACK THOSE CLAMS!"

"...AND HERE WE HAVE MR. AMERICA."

"SONJA HATES CRAZY SHIRLEY."

"YOU'RE RIGHT!...IT IS A SNOWBIRD!"

"HE'S PLANNING A BACK FENCE JAZZ FESTIVAL!"

"EVER SEE SPIKE TEAR A PHONE BOOK IN HALF ?!"

"EVER SEE HEATHCLIFF SHRED ONE ?!"

"I WISH HE WOULDN'T TAILGATE!"

"CRAZY SHIRLEY."

"GO UP THERE AND WATCH LIKE EVERYBODY ELSE!"

"HEATHCLIFF, I HOPE YOU'RE NOT ANNOYING THE PLUMBER!"

"HOW'D YOU MANAGE TO GET BABY FOOD ALL OVER THIS?!"

"STOPPING IN FOR THE BUSINESS MAN'S LUNCH ?!"

"THREE MINUTES FOR CRAZY SHIRLEY!"

"PLEASE DON'T FEEL YOU HAVE TO ENTERTAIN US!!"

"NO, NO, CHAUNCY!"

"ET TU, BRUTÈ P!"

"MIND IF I SMOKE?"

"THAT'S MY GOOD BOY!... ALWAYS ON THE JOB,
CHABING MICE."

"AREN'T YOU A LITTLE OUT OF SEASON ?!"

"COMMUTING?"

"PLEASE TELL CRAZY SHIRLEY SHE'S FORGIVEN!"

"...SO LOOK FOR 'WHOOPEE LIVER LUMPS' IN THE BRIGHT YELLOW CAN!"

"NOT BAD, BUT WILL VENTRILOQUISM SELL CATFOOD?"

"IT'S HIS NEW FAVORITE...TUNA TACOS!"

"I'M FED UP WITH HIS SERENADES!"

"I'D LIKE TO MAKE HEATHCLIFF A COAT, BUT I DON'T HAVE THE RIGHT SIZE DUMMY."

"HOW 'BOUT THIS BASKETBALL?"

"THEY CLAIM IF WE TALK TO OUR PLANTS,
IT HELPS THEM GROW."

"IT'S FOR YOU."

"THEY'RE GETTING MORE BRAZEN THAN EVER!"

"GRIND UP TWO OF THESE IN YOUR TUNA FISH."

"HE'S IN THE BACKYARD ANNOYING MY SCOTTY!"

"CRAZY SHIRLEY'S DIARY BROUGHT A NICE PRICE!"

"HEATHCLIFF IS GIVING CHAUNCY A TONGUE DEPRESSOR FOR HIS BIRTHDAY."

"CHAUNCY JUST LOVES RECEIVING GIFTS!"

"YOUR MECHANICAL MOUSE HAS BEEN RECALLED BY DETROIT."

"HE SPLIT FIVE SIGNS!... I WONDER
IF THAT'S A RECORD?"

"WITH FISH, WE GENERALLY RECOMMEND A WHITE WINE."

"HE DOESN'T LIKE TO SEE THEM STANDING AROUND THE WATER COOLER."

"HAVE YOU BEEN AT THAT BIRD BATH AGAIN?!"

"YOUR BLOCKS??...I THINK YOU LEFT THEM
IN THE KITCHEN."

" WATCH OUT!...

...IT'S CRAZY SHIRLEY!"

"YOUR BACK FENCE PARTIES ARE GETTING OUT OF HAND!"

"BE CAREFUL, DEAR... I JUST WAXED."

"FRITZ! DON'T START ANYTHING!"

"AUF WIEDERSEHEN."

"IT SEEMS HE HAS LARYNGITIS."

"HEATHCLIFF WOULD LIKE IT GIFT WRAPPED."

"GRANDPA, HEATHCLIFF MADE YOU A TIE RACK!"

"SINCE WHEN DO WE CARRY GARBAGE CANS SIDEWAYS?"

"I DON'T WANT TO DISTURB HIS AFTER DINNER NAP."

"ORDINARILY, I WOULDN'T EVEN KNOW IT WAS OPENING NIGHT AT THE OPERA!"

"I'M AFRAID, SIR, THAT IT HAS COOED ITS LAST COO."

"ONCE IN A WHILE, I WOULDN'T MIND
A SHRIMP COCKTAIL, MYSELF!"

"HE'S INTO PUNK ROCK!"

"AS USUAL, HE'S CONCERNED ABOUT THE TUNA FLEET."

"AS SOON AS I GET OVER THIS COLD, WE CAN PLAY 'DOLL CARRIAGE' AGAIN."

"WE DON'T ACCEPT TRADE-INS."

" CRAZY SHIRLEY'S BRIDGE CLUB. "

"I'M NOT GOING TO ARGUE WITH YOU!"

"FANG!.... HERE, FANG!!"

© 1978 McNaught Synd. Inc.

"UMMM?... ERRR?... THANKS A LOT."

"COME VISIT US AGAIN, SOON!...

....AND BRING YOUR DACHSHUND."

"...STYLING, SHAMPOO, FLUFF DRYING, FACIAL, BATH, PEDICURE, CLIPPING AND TRIM...THAT COMES TO..."

"HAPPY EASTER."

"DID YOU HEAR THE NEWS?...SPIKE IS A FATHER!"

"WILL YOU GET HIM OUTA HERE ?!!"

"OH, WOW! IT'S A BIG BEAUTY!"

"WHOOPS!"

"GIVE ME THAT LIFE PRESERVER!"

"FRANKLY, HEATHCLIFF, I'VE NEVER CARED MUCH
FOR LAWN ORNAMENTS."

"I'M ANXIOUS TO SEE HOW CHAUNCY DOES
IN OBEDIENCE SCHOOL!"

"JUST MAKE YOURSELF RIGHT AT HOME."

"CRAZY SHIRLEY HATES STRAINED SPINACH!"

"HE SEEMS TO ENJOY THE GAME!"

"...FURTHERMORE, I PREDICT A BANNER YEAR
FOR 'WHOOPEE CAT FOOD.'..."

"WE DON'T PUT MASCOTS ON BUBBLEGUM CARDS."

"GESUNDHEIT!"

© 1978
McNaught Synd., Inc.

4-6

"YOUR SATIN SHEETS ARE AT THE CLEANERS."

"HE'S ADDED AN USHER!"

"SOMEONE TRIED TO GET AT OUR OCTOPUS
AND OUR PENGUINS!"

"WHERE HAVE YOU BEEN ?!"

"I'M LOOKING FOR A NEW TRUCK, ED."

" HAVE YOU SEEN HEATHCLIFF ?...
HE WAS CHASING A DACHSHUND."

"OH, SWELL!"

"HAH!...SHADOW BOXING WON'T HELP
WHEN YOU'RE GOING UP AGAINST SPIKE!"

"I HAVE THE FEELING THAT I'M BEING SET UP!"

"I'M TELLIN' YA.... HE'S THROWING A SPITBALL!"

"NOW YOU'LL HAVE TO BE CHANGED!"

"OTHER THAN THAT, HOW DO YOU LIKE IT?"

" SIXTH FLOOR...ACE CAT FOOD, INC.."

"OH-OH!...LOOKS LIKE CHOIR PRACTICE TONIGHT!"

"IT'S FOR HIS GIRLFRIEND...WOULD YOU GIFTWRAP IT?"

"HE'S TIRED OF LOOKING AT THE SAME OLD MAGAZINES!"

"HERE COMES CRAZY SHIRLEY...

...AND THERE GOES 'KISSING ROCK'!"

"WHAT HAVE YOU DONE WITH THE BABY POWDER?!"

"TIRED OF THE OLD RAT-RACE ?"